GETTING TO KNOW
THE U.S. PRESIDENTS

JAMES
MONROE

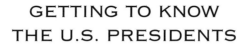

FIFTH PRESIDENT
1817 – 1825

WRITTEN AND ILLUSTRATED BY MIKE VENEZIA

CHILDREN'S PRESS®
A DIVISION OF SCHOLASTIC INC.
NEW YORK   TORONTO   LONDON   AUCKLAND   SYDNEY
MEXICO CITY   NEW DELHI   HONG KONG
DANBURY, CONNECTICUT

Reading Consultant: Nanci R. Vargus, Ed.D., Assistant Professor, School of Education, University of Indianapolis

Historical Consultant: Marc J. Selverstone, Ph.D., Assistant Professor, Miller Center of Public Affairs, University of Virginia

Photographs © 2004:
Art Resource, NY: 3 (National Portrait Gallery, Smithsonian Institution, Washington, D.C.), 12
Ash-Lawn Highland: 18
Bridgeman Art Library International Ltd., London/New York: 28 (Christie's Images/Private Collection), 7 (Victoria & Albert Museum, London, UK)
Corbis Images: 10, 11 (Archivo Iconografico, S.A.), 20, 26 (Bettmann)
General Mills, Inc. via SODA: 32
Library of Congress, Prints and Photographs Division: 14
North Wind Picture Archives: 6, 16, 25
Superstock, Inc.: 17

Colorist for illustrations: Dave Ludwig

Library of Congress Cataloging-in-Publication Data

Venezia, Mike.
   James Monroe / written and illustrated by Mike Venezia.
      p. cm. — (Getting to know the U.S. presidents)
   Summary: An introduction to the life of James Monroe, an influential patriot during the American Revolution who became the nation's fifth president and was subsequently reelected.
   ISBN 0-516-22610-X (lib. bdg.)   0-516-27479-1 (pbk.)
   1. Monroe, James, 1758-1831—Juvenile literature. 2. Presidents—United States—Biography—Juvenile literature. [1. Monroe, James, 1758-1831. 2. Presidents.] I. Title.
   E372.V46 2004
   973.5'4'092—dc22

                              2003016005

13 14 15 R 13 12

James Monroe was the fifth president of the United States. He was born in the colony of Virginia in 1758. As a young man, James was a war hero. He served under General George Washington during the Revolutionary War.

Of the first five U.S. presidents—George Washington, John Adams, Thomas Jefferson, James Madison, and James Monroe—four were from Virginia. Only John Adams was from another state, Massachusetts.

Being a Virginian caused James Monroe some problems when he ran for president. People from other states were beginning to feel left out. Even so, James Monroe was popular enough to be elected president twice.

An illustration showing George Washington on his plantation in Virginia

Just like George Washington, Thomas Jefferson, and James Madison, James Monroe grew up on a large farm called a plantation. On plantations, slaves from Africa were forced to plant and harvest tobacco, cotton, or other crops.

James never talked much about his childhood. He must have learned to hunt, shoot, and ride horses, though. He used these skills well when he was a soldier. James probably explored the wilderness areas around his family's plantation, too. The Virginia countryside was filled with forests and wild animals. Many American Indians lived there, too.

A view of the Virginia countryside in the 1700s

James Monroe had an excellent education.
In grade school, his favorite subjects were
Latin and math. James also liked to race.
He had a few contests with a classmate of his
named John Marshall. John Marshall became
the chief justice of the United States Supreme
Court when he grew up.

When James was sixteen years old, his father
died. His mother died a few months later.
James' wealthy uncle, Judge Joseph Jones, helped
the Monroe family out during this sad time.
He made sure James continued his education.
In 1774, James Monroe entered William and
Mary College in Williamsburg, Virginia.

While James Monroe was growing up, Virginia was one of thirteen colonies in North America ruled by Great Britain and King George III. Whenever the British government needed more money, the king would add charges, called taxes, to products the colonists needed. The colonists had no say in the matter.

An old map of the world

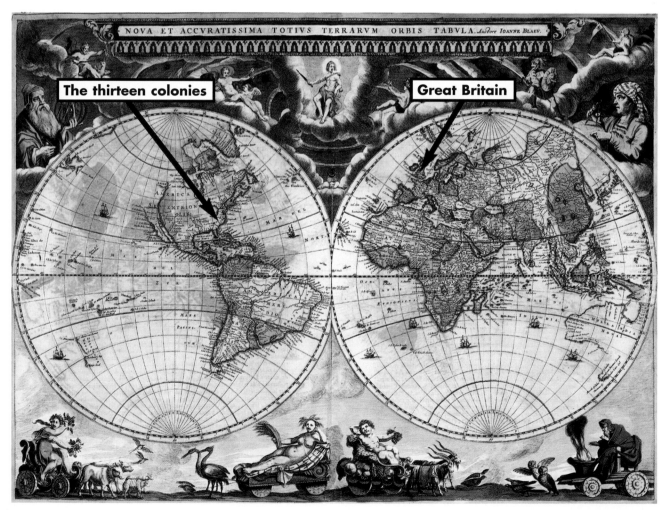

A portrait of George III,
by Thomas Gainsborough

The king also did other things that were unpleasant. He sent British soldiers to the colonies to make sure the taxes were being paid. Sometimes colonists who were accused of crimes were found guilty without a fair trial. The colonists were not happy with the way they were being bossed around.

Some battles broke out between British soldiers and the colonists in 1775. Finally, the leaders of the colonies decided to break away from their English rulers and become an independent country. In 1776, a Declaration of Independence was announced. In college, James Monroe was learning all about England's unfair treatment of the colonists. James decided to join Virginia's militia.

In 1775, the Revolutionary War began when fighting broke out between colonists and British soldiers in Lexington, Massachusetts.

Militias were volunteer military groups formed to defend people against the British army. James attended school during the day, but at night he was sometimes active in the militia. One time, he and a bunch of other students carried out a dangerous raid on the arsenal at the British governor's mansion in Williamsburg. They took muskets, gunpowder, and other items they needed to defend themselves.

James Monroe was among the soldiers who crossed the Delaware River with General George Washington (on white horse) in 1776.

When James was only seventeen years old, he decided to leave college and join General George Washington's Continental Army. Right away, he began fighting in battles that took place in and around New York City. One of them took place in what is today Central Park!

On Christmas Day 1776, James was with General Washington when he made his famous crossing of the Delaware River to attack enemies in Trenton, New Jersey.

James Monroe was seriously wounded during this battle and returned to Virginia to recover. General Washington was so proud of James' bravery that he promoted him to the rank of captain.

James was excited to have a chance to command his own group of soldiers. The only problem was that there were hardly any men around to command. Everyone was either under someone else's command or trying to stay out of the army.

The British army surrendering to General Washington at Yorktown

James Monroe fought bravely in other battles during the Revolutionary War. Finally, in 1781, the British army gave up, and a peace treaty was signed in 1783. General Washington's army had won the war. The American colonies were officially a new country: the United States of America. James was only twenty-three when the war ended.

Because of his intelligence, gentle personality, bravery, and handsome good looks, James Monroe was well liked. During the war, he had served as a military assistant to Virginia's governor, Thomas Jefferson. He also

studied law with Jefferson. James and Thomas got along really well. Jefferson helped James Monroe begin an exciting career serving his new country.

A portrait of Thomas Jefferson by Charles Peale Polk

A portrait of Elizabeth Monroe
during the 1790s

James was always being asked to attend meetings or serve on important committees that represented his state. During a trip to New York, James met a girl named Elizabeth Kortright. After dating for a while, they fell in love and got married. As busy as James was, he still found time to travel.

James Monroe wanted to see the beautiful rugged mountains, wildlife, and rushing rivers to the west of the newly formed United States. James talked to settlers and learned about their hopes and concerns. James always believed that the awesome wilderness areas he saw should be part of the United States some day.

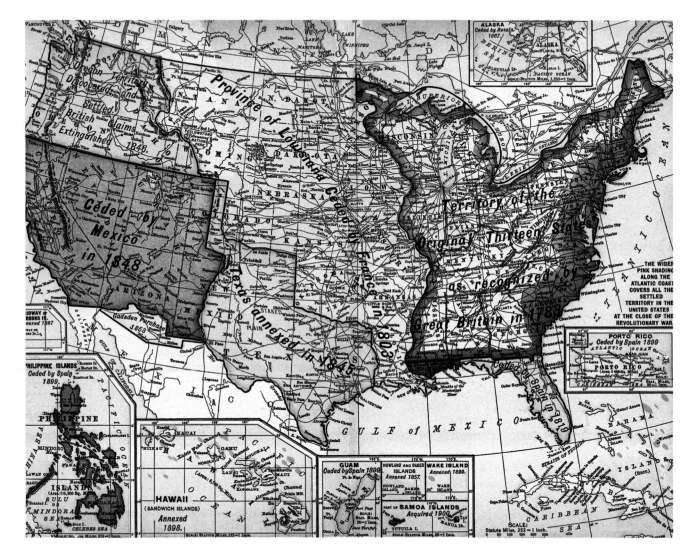

This map shows when various territories became U.S. land. In 1783, the nation owned only the eastern third of what is today the United States. In 1803, James Monroe helped make the deal to buy the Louisiana Territory (yellow area), which almost doubled the size of the United States.

When Thomas Jefferson became president, he asked James Monroe to travel to France. Jefferson wanted to see if the United States could buy the important shipping port of New Orleans, which belonged to France at that time.

When he arrived, James was surprised to learn that the French were interested in selling not only New Orleans, but also a huge area of land called the Louisiana Territory. In 1803, James Monroe and another American, Robert Livingston, worked out a deal to buy almost a million square miles of land. The Louisiana Purchase almost doubled the size of the United States, just like that!

James didn't have much luck, though, when he traveled to Spain to see if the United States could buy Florida. This area, owned by the Spanish king, would have been an important addition for the United States, too. However, Spain wouldn't consider selling it until years later, after James Monroe became president.

James returned to the United States in 1808. A few years later, he helped his country get through its second war with England, the War of 1812. For years, the British had been stopping American ships and forcing American sailors to join their navy. When the British refused to stop, the two countries went to war.

Since 1811, James Monroe had been doing a great job as secretary of state under President James Madison. During the war, he helped out even more by also becoming secretary of war.

In 1814, British troops marched into and burned Washington, D.C.

The war didn't go very well for the United States. At one point, British soldiers marched into Washington, D.C., and almost burned it to the ground.

The Americans kept fighting, though, and by the end of 1814, they had managed to battle the British to a draw.

James Monroe helped with the peace talks that ended the War of 1812. Unfortunately, the talks were held in Europe, and before anyone back in the United States got the good news, there was one last battle. The U.S. Army, led by General Andrew Jackson, beat the British in what became known as the Battle of New Orleans. Many lives were lost in a battle that never should have happened.

An engraving showing the Battle of New Orleans

When President Madison's term ended, James Monroe decided to run for president. Monroe won the election and began his new job in 1817. When James and Elizabeth moved into the president's house, it was being repaired and painted white to cover up the ugly burn marks left from the war. It soon became known as the White House.

Picking Cotton, by William Aiken Walker

James Monroe had lots of problems to face when he started out as president. One of the biggest problems the United States had to deal with was slavery. Most people in the North were against slavery, but people in the South used slaves to run their plantations.

Even plantation owners who believed that slavery was cruel and unfair owned slaves, including James Monroe. James worked on a plan to slow down or stop slavery in any new states that were added to the nation. He also worked to keep an equal number of free states and slave states in the nation. This plan was called the Missouri Compromise. This compromise helped keep the disagreement over slavery from getting too out of hand until 1861, when the Civil War began.

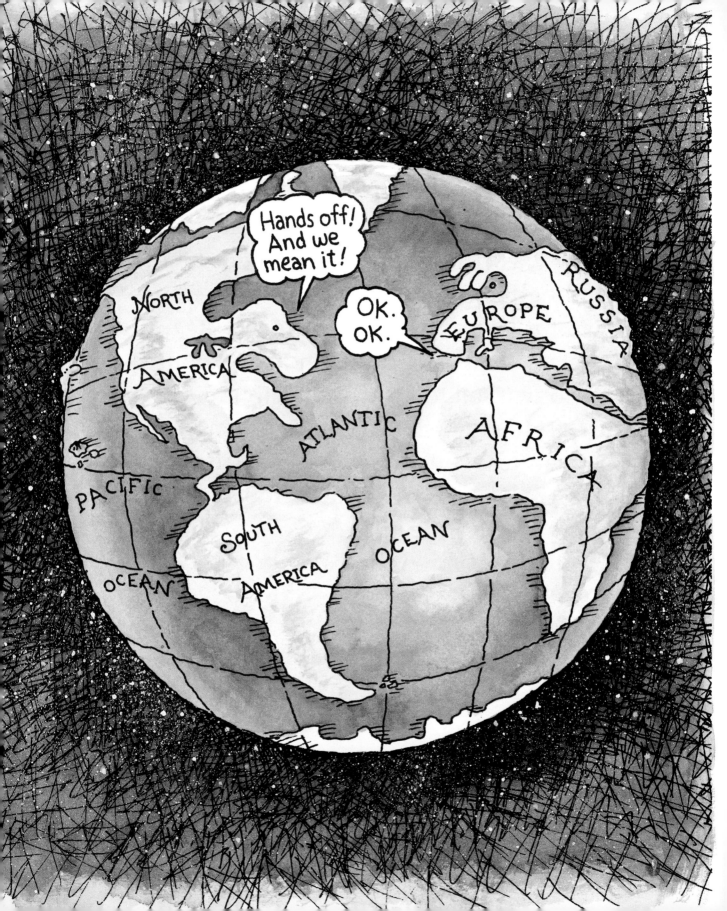

During his second term, President Monroe had to deal with another big problem. He learned that a bunch of European countries offered to help Spain reclaim some colonies it had once ruled in Central America and South America. James Monroe didn't want any European leaders interfering in areas that were so close to the United States.

President Monroe and his secretary of state, John Quincy Adams, wrote a strong message to the world that later became known as the Monroe Doctrine. It said that if any European country messed around with South America, Central America, or North America, the United States would be willing to go to war to stop them. In return for Europe's cooperation, the United States promised to stay out of Europe's business.

James Monroe was such a popular president that no one wanted to run against him when he was up for re-election. During his two terms, James did whatever he could to help his country grow. He saw his country expand to include twenty-four states. He encouraged the building of roads and canals to connect new states with the original ones.

James Monroe retired in 1825 and returned to Virginia. After his wife died in 1830, Monroe went to live with a daughter in New York. James Monroe died at the age of seventy-three on July 4, 1831. That day happened to be the fifty-fifth anniversary of the approval of the Declaration of Independence.